Hair to Dye For

A Hair Colorist's Secrets Revealed

Penny Baptista

iUniverse, Inc.
New York   Bloomington

Hair to Dye For
A Hair Colorist's Secrets Revealed

iUniverse books may be ordered through booksellers or by contacting:

iUniverse
1663 Liberty Drive
Bloomington, IN 47403
www.iuniverse.com
1-800-Authors (1-800-288-4677)

ISBN: 978-0-595-52483-9 (pbk)
ISBN: 978-0-595-62536-9 (ebk)

Printed in the United States of America

iUniverse rev. date: 1/7/2009

A Word of Thanks

Oprah said something on her TV show years ago that really stuck with me and started me on the path to writing this book. The episode was about self-made millionaires who had made a career out of doing what they loved. Hearing Oprah's simple advice, "Do what you know" was the light bulb moment that inspired me to write this book on hair color. I want to thank Oprah for her wise words that helped me follow my passion.

Contents

Acknowledgments	ix
About the Author	xi
Introduction to Hair Color	1
Levels and Tones	6
Developers	11
Toners and Other Colors	15
Applications	19
Creative Applications	23
Going Green	26
Scalp Treatments, Disorders, and Diseases	32
Hair Color Corrections	36
Product Knowledge	41
Salon Styles	45
Final Thought	49
GLOSSARY	50

Acknowledgments

I have many people to thank for their continued support over the years and for believing in me:

My mom, Shirley Louise, for her love. She is my biggest fan, my cheerleader, my best friend, and the wind beneath my wings.

My brothers, John and Joel, Aunt Clella, and Uncle Tom for their love and guidance.

My best and dear friends Lynn, Melissa, Betty, Vicki, Linda, Esther, and Melody.

Tony for the tech work and Melody for her help with the manuscript.

Patty for her motivation, for getting me on the path of being a stylist, and for being a dear friend.

Sue for the early work on the book and her great ideas.

My colleagues Francis, Caroline, Charles, George, Linnette,

Linda, Remi, and Miguel, with whom I have worked for many years. We have shared laughter and fun times. Some of us have been together for over two decades.

All the loyal clients who have been with me through the many changes in my life. They have helped me become the success I am today. By letting me try new styles and colors and express my creativity, they motivate me to be the best I can be.

God, the light in my life and the power that made this all come together.

About the Author

Penny Baptista has been an award-winning stylist and hair color specialist for more than twenty years. Her salons in Pacific Heights and Russian Hill cater to San Francisco's elite and attract clients from across the country. Penny has also worked part-time as an educator for Clairol, taught Logics hair color workshops to other stylists and salon owners across northern California, and worked in hair shows behind the scenes as well as on stage. Semi retired at this point in her career, she looks forward to expanding her expertise to include the field of cosmetology.

Introduction to Hair Color

HAIR COLORING IS NOT an idea that is new to us. It has been around for thousands of years, but people had to be a little bit more creative in ancient times. Egyptians made hair dye from the leaves from various plants, including henna, indigo, chamomile, and sage. A royal formula dating from 1200 BC used dried tadpoles mixed with oil and tortoise shells. They were certainly creative for the time. Then around the 1500s both Hennas and Indigo were used as hair dies. *Indigofera Tinctoria* is a plant native to India. A blue dye obtained from this plant was used as a die called Indigo.

Henna is an old world plant called *Lawsonia Inermis,* with its small red and white flowers having the fragrance of roses. The dye was extracted from the leaves of the plant for hair color. Even certain teas and fruit juices were used as well. Even today Hennas are very popular in the hair color industry.

Things have come a long way since the early days of hair color. Today it's a billion-dollar industry and one of the most popular salon services. Whether you are the do-it- yourself type or a professional stylist, I am here to walk you through the process of achieving salon beautiful hair.

Both men and women are turning to hair color for many reasons. Some wish to banish their grays, while others seek to brighten up a drab natural color. Many people are attracted to the special effects that hair color can bring. Hair coloring gives a variety of results, from conditioning the hair to expanding the actual hair shaft. Each strand of hair can double in size, making hair thicker. I knew someone who used to color her hair using permanent color, just to increase the thickness of her fine, limp hair.

Hair color can be divided into five categories based on the way the color affects the hair: temporary, semi permanent and demi permanent, permanent, high lift, and natural organic colors.

Let's start with the temporary hair colors that are applied after shampooing and left on as a treatment. Some rinse out with one shampoo. They enhance natural hair color and come in liquids, gels, and mousses. Personally, I like the mousse, but if you use the liquid, put it in a spray bottle. It makes for a much easier, more even application. It's safe for natural blonds, but those with highlighted hair should be cautious of these products. Do a patch test, because the dye may grab on to the porous hair and not rinse out. I had a nightmare experience with this while in cosmetology school. I used an enhancing shampoo to enhance my highlights. When I got out of the shower, I had fuchsia pink hair. Remember to be cautious if your hair is pre-lightened. If you have virgin hair (hair that's never had chemicals on it), temporary dyes are a stress-free way to try colors, because they just shampoo out. However, excessive use of this product can cause buildup. You may have seen people with a green or purple cast to their hair. This is a result of the base color of the product. If you are trying to cover gray, don't use it. Instead, use a semi permanent or permanent color. Remember, this product is only a rinse and should be used to enhance color, not to cover gray.

Semi permanent and demi permanent hair colors are pretty much the same. Demi permanent is a little stronger. It colors the hair by coating it and penetrates slightly into the hair shaft. A semi-permanent hair color will last through several shampoos before slowly fading away. The hair color usually lasts four to six weeks, depending on how often you shampoo. There is no lifting action, which means it won't lighten your hair; it's deposit-only hair color. Manufacturers say it's not for gray coverage because they can't guarantee it will work, but I have found it to be wonderfully effective in helping to blend the gray away by enhancing the natural color. It has proven to be a good product for checking out new shades without the commitment of out growth and roots. You will usually find beautiful browns, reds, and chestnut colors in the semi or demi colors. If your pre- lightened hair is in the blond family and is looking faded or brassy, semi colors work very well when used as a toner. Semi and demi colors also bring condition, shine, and bounce back to overstressed hair. When using semi-permanent color, use one shade lighter than suggested on the box, bottle, or tube. In my experience, it is wise to go a level lighter, because there is no lifting action like you would find in permanent hair colors. When using semi- and demi-permanent hair colors you will be using 5–10 volume developers.

A permanent hair color colors the hair by penetrating through the cuticle into the cortex layer of the hair. This method keeps the hair color from washing out. This hair color will stay in the hair until it grows out or is cut out; permanent color has 100 percent gray coverage. You will also have the obligation of doing regular touch-ups on the outgrowth. If you're going to use this product, it's a little bit more of a commitment than the others. When using this product you will be using 20–40 volume developers. Use 20- volume developer for gray coverage and 30–40 for lighter shades and highlights.

High-lift hair colors are the blonds of the group. They are usually mixed with 30–40 volume developers. For hair that is more than 75 percent gray and wants to go blond, use 20 or 30 volume developer. Black or very dark hair you probably requires a 40 volume developer However, dark brown or black hair that doesn't lighten enough may need bleach to break up the pigment of the hair, then a toner to achieve the desired result.

Powdered lighteners and bleaches are used when no pigment is wanted in the hair. They are the strongest of all color compounds and can be the most damaging. Use extreme caution. They come in powder form and can be used on or off the scalp. When doing bleach touch-ups, be careful not to overlap the bleach with any pre-lightened hair; this could cause breakage. When doing an application on virgin hair, you may need more than one application to achieve your desired result. You can use a 20- volume developer for this process. When doing highlights, you can use 30- volume developer. As the hair gets lighter, its porosity increases, so the hair's moisture will escape more easily. It is important to use a penetrating conditioner to replace the moisture lost in the lightening process. It will also help to close the cuticle of the hair. When a lightener is used on very dark hair, it will go through various stages: black to brown to red to red gold to gold to yellow to pale yellow. The pale yellow color closely resembles the inside of a banana peel. When lightening the hair, remember that you are stripping its natural pigment and making it vulnerable to extreme heat. Snarls and tangles should be removed very carefully. I highly recommend that you use a leave-in conditioner after shampooing the hair.

Quiz

1. What is the difference between semi- permanent and demi-permanent hair color?

2. What is the difference between semi-permanent and permanent hair color?

3. What can happen when bleach is overlapped on pre-bleached hair?

4. What is the process for getting rid of too much buildup on overly colored hair that's darker in one section?

5. What is a temporary hair color?

Answers

1. Semi- permanent and demi- permanent colors are very similar; however, demi- permanent is stronger than semi-permanent.

2. Semi- permanent color will rinse out over time, but permanent hair color will not.

3. Major damage can result if too much bleach is overlapped, it will cause breakage.

4. Mix bleach with 20- volume developer, and brush it on the section that is too dark. Watch and wait until the color is lifted just a shade or two. Wash out the mixture and dry the hair. Proceed with color. Start with the root area, then continue coloring the rest of the hair. Leave on for thirty minutes. You can also use a hair color remover.

5. Temporary color rinses out with the first shampoo.

NOTES

$\mathcal{L}$evels and Tones

COLOR DEPTH IS MEASURED in levels. The level is the degree from dark to light, from black hair to blond hair and all the beautiful hair colors in between. This chapter will cover how to determine hair's natural level, how to achieve the desired level, and the final result. The amount of pigment in the hair determines the depth of color. Most people are in the middle of the chart from medium brown to medium blond, levels 4–7. Most of the colors I do in the salon are around these levels. Once you understand the level of color, you can buy any color line. Knowing what level you are and knowing the chart is helpful in choosing the correct color. Color swatches are available at most beauty supply stores. Pick out the color swatch that most resembles your hair. Looking in a mirror, fan out the swatch, and overlap it with your hair. If you can't tell the difference, it's a match and you now know your level for that hair color line and most of the other color lines, which usually follow this same format for labeling their colors. Knowing that I am a level 6 makes it easy when buying a hair color formula from a manufacturer I am not familiar with. This formula is the basic foundation for the majority of hair color lines:

1 black
2 darkest brown
3 dark brown
4 medium brown
5 light brown
6 dark blond
7 medium blond
8 light blond
9 very light blond
10 lightest blond
11–12 high-lift blonds

Knowing that black is level 1 and the lightest blond is level 10 gives you an idea of how the level system works.

The other important term used in hair color is *tone*, which indicates the tonal value of the color and whether it is a warm tone or a cool tone. The different tones are gold, red, violet, blue, and green. Gold tones are used on blonds, and golden browns warm up drab hair and make beautiful highlights. Gold mixed with violet creates a neutral formula that colors gray beautifully.

Red tones have a variety of colors from coppery red to cool red, depending on the other tones you use with it. Red by itself is bright red; mixed with gold it gives a coppery red, while mixed with a violet base, it produces a cool Irish setter red, and mixed with a blue base it turns to auburn. If your hair is too red and you want to tone it down, use a blue base color to cut the warmth and use a shade darker than your hair.

Violet shades are cool shades. Ash or beige colors have a violet base. Violet will neutralize gold tones in the hair. Violet tones are warmer than blue tones even though both are cool. Mixed with golden tones, violet gives a neutral formula, so it makes a great toner for hair that has too much gold. A level 10, hair color with a violet base and a 5- volume developer for bleached blonds will tone down unwanted brassy tones and even out the hair color.

Blue tones should not be used alone or on gray or blond hair. Do not use them on permanent waved hair either. Mixing with blue with gold creates a green base hair color formula. The blue neutralizes unwanted red tones.

Green tones neutralize unwanted red tones. They are best when mixed with other tones. Do not use green base color alone.

Neutral tones are the perfect blend of the primary colors red, blue, and yellow. They cover gray 100 percent on all levels. Neutral can be used on gray and pigmented hair; it adds a rich, natural tone. For gray coverage when using other tones, mix one- fourth ounce neutral into the color formula. Neutrals are the most used tone in the hair color line, because you can use them by themselves or mixed with other tones to create new colors. Most importantly, remember that violet tones neutralize unwanted gold tones and blue and green tones neutralize unwanted red tones. So the base of all hair color is levels and tones. Knowing this will help in all aspects of the hair color process.

Abbreviations on packaging indicate tone:

R = red
C = copper
G = gold
N = neutral
V =violet
B = blue
G = green
RV = red and violet
RC = red and copper
RG = red and gold
RO = red and orange
RB = red and blue
BV = blue and violet.

You get the idea of how the abbreviations are used in the color line. There are probably other combinations with different color lines; however, these are the most popular. By mixing RV and RC (or RO) you get a beautiful Irish setter red in a level 4–6. With R or C and N, you get auburn in levels 4–6. R and G in levels 6–8, strawberry blond. G and N with levels 4–7 produces a warm brown. R and V and N in levels 3–5 chestnut brown. There are many combinations mixing different tones together, a great colorist is creative and daring so go for it!

Mixing these colors sometimes calls for equal parts and sometimes calls for adding one-fourth of an ounce, most often with the reds. Use one-fourth ounce N (neutral) to any formula to mellow it out a little and to ensure gray coverage. Mixing and being a chemist is the fun part of doing hair color. Don't be afraid to mix different tones to achieve different hair colors, you can also use some of the tones alone and get beautiful results. Don't be afraid to mix it up you may find a beautiful color that you never thought of. By putting together tones you were unsure of.

Quiz

1. What are levels?
2. What is the tonality of the hair?
3. If the hair's natural level is 6 with a touch of gray, what color should be used to dye it auburn?
4. What is used to get the red tone out of hair?
5. What is used to get the brassiness out of blond hair?
6. What level is black?

Answers

1. Levels are the degree from dark to light.
2. Tones are the coolness and warmth of a color.
3. Try not to think of hair colors as words written on a package. Instead, think of them in tones. For this example, use a level 6 and have it be a red tone with one half ounce of 6 N (neutral). 6RC or 6RO/ with N, with 20-volume developer.
4. Use a blue-toned color a shade darker than the hair.
5. Use a violet-toned color a shade darker.
6. Level 1.

NOTES

Developers

DEVELOPERS AND GENERATORS ARE the chemical compound that bonds the hair color to the hair. It's the chemical combination of the hair color and the developer that makes the products work. Without this combination, the color would not adhere to the hair shaft. Developers and generators either deposit or strip color from the hair, depending on their degree of strength. They have many uses and come in liquid or cream form; I personally prefer the cream form. When the developer mixes with the hair color, the oxidation process starts. It takes approximately thirty to forty-five minutes to color the hair once the mixture has been applied. You cannot save the mixed color and reuse it, because the oxidation process has already been completed and the color will no longer do its work.

Oxidation is a chemical reaction in which hydrogen peroxide releases oxygen when it is mixed with the color ingredients found in liquid or cream tints. A developer or activator is made of hydrogen peroxide, a chemical composed of two parts oxygen and two parts hydrogen. With the combination of hair color developer and air, the process of oxidation starts, and you will notice the hair darkening. Be patient; the oxidation process always looks darker than the end result.

You will see different volumes of developers at the store. The volume of developer has different results on the hair and tint it is mixed with. For diluting other developers, use a 0 volume developer. You can mix 0 volume with 30 volume to get 25 volume. Mix a 10 volume developer with a 0 volume to produce a 5 volume developer. Use 5 volume developers for deposit only hair colors, such as semi-permanent colors and toners.

A 10- volume developer is a deposit-only developer, like 5volume. It has no lifting action, meaning it doesn't lighten the hair. It usually is found in semi or demi permanent hair colors. There is no guarantee it will cover gray hair, but it has better results when placed under a dryer. It also makes a good toner for blond and hair that is too brassy. Mix with level 10- hair color violet base.

A 20- volume developer has little lifting action and is good for gray coverage. It's also good for using on virgin hair for a total color change.

A 30- volume developer is a medium-lift developer. You can use it on the scalp for blond formulas level 6–10 and for highlights as well.

A 40- volume developer is for high lifting, when you want allover blond or highlights. It's the strongest of the developers.

The 50–60 volume developers are rumored to exist, but I haven't seen them. If you locate these, remember that they are for high-lift tints and that they are very strong.

If you need a toner and don't have one, you can use any permanent hair color with 5- volume developer. It's a good idea to always have a 0 volume developer available in your lab to turn any color into a toner. This will work in a pinch if needed, but best to use a semi, demi, or toner.

0- volume developer is for diluting other developers.

5- volume developer for deposit in semi and demi permanent, for priming (about priming page 37), and permanent colors.

10- volume developer for deposit in semi and demi and permanent colors.

20- volume developers for permanent colors and gray coverage.

30- volume developers for permanent and blond formulas.

40- volume developers for high lift blonds and highlights.

50 and 60- volume developers the highest of lift of all developers.

Quiz

1. What is a developer?

2. How is a 5-volume developer made?

3. When is a 20-volume developer used?

4. What volume developer is used to produce a very blond color?

5. What volume developer should be used to deposit color with no lift?

Answers

1. It is the chemical that adheres the hair color to the hair. It's made of two parts oxygen and two parts hydrogen.

2. Mix equal parts of 10 volume developer and 0 volume developer.

3. For allover hair color and for covering gray.

4. Use 40-volume developer.

5. Use either 5 or 10 volume developer.

NOTES

Toners and Other Colors

TONERS ARE USED TO tone down any unwanted hair color. Even back in the day when being bleached blond was popular, colorists followed the bleaching process with a toner. Whether it was for an ashy beige blond or a golden blond, toners have always been used. They are a great way to add tonality to any hair color. If your hair is a drab brown, for instance, you may want to use a coppery red toner just to see if you like it, because it rinses out after a while. Toners are usually mixed with a 5-volume developer, but there are some products to apply directly to the hair with no developer. If you are in need of a toner, look around to see what best suits you. Fanciful is a rinse and is used as a leave-in product. I still consider Fanciful a toner. It comes in either liquid or mousse form. If you use the liquid, I suggest putting it in a spray bottle for even application. This product will cause buildup, which can be treated with a color remover. I like the mousse form, because it's easy to apply. Depending on the product, use gloves when applying. Make sure to do a patch test to check for allergies and to see if you like the shade. Some color mousses may need to be rinsed out, so make sure you read the directions.

There is another trend in hair color that is popular with young and creative types, there is Manic Panic and 'N Rage. I am sure there are more brands out there, but these are the ones I have seen and used. They come in brilliant shades: blues, turquoise, pinks, hot reds, apple greens, and all the colors in between. Sometimes you can apply them on virgin hair and it will look great, but most times pre-lightening is required for spectacular results. Some products work like a stain, and others you may need to mix with an activator. Just look at the instructions before purchasing. Streak & Tip is a line of spray-on hair colors mainly used around Halloween and is fun to use for that quick shot of color. Be careful with pre-lightened or natural blond hair the color may stain, and you will need to get color remover to get out. A strand test is the best advice I can give you. Dye just a small section of hair and look at the results before committing color to the whole head.

Jazzing is a great product. It's a glaze, a translucent color, and it adds shine. There are two ways to use this product. One way is to apply and leave on for five to fifteen minutes before washing it out. The second way is to place a cap over the product, place your head under a dryer, and, depending on the depth of color needed, check it after fifteen minutes. This product is fine for chemically treated hair, whether permanent waved, colored, or relaxed. Because this kind of hair is porous, make sure you check it thoroughly throughout the process. Rub a piece of the colored hair on a towel to check results.

Cellophanes are also a product that adds shine and condition. It is applied on the hair before setting under the dryer. It is a translucent color and comes in various shades. It is good for chemically treated hair to add tonality and as a glaze for the hair. I am sure there are other glazes out there, but I haven't tried them all. When you want to try a glaze, take time to explore what's available.

Ardel is a hair color enhancer; it comes in a clear option to add shine and deeper colors to enhance dark brown to black hair. It's a great product if your hair is faded and needs some richness. Some good shades are mahogany, plum rose, and cinnamon.

There are so many different hair color companies that it would take a separate book just to list them all. Go ahead buy a few, experiment, and have fun. Remember if you are the slightest bit unsure do a test strand to make sure you and your client will like it. Don't rush the process, because it can take more time in the end if it comes out wrong.

Quiz

1. What is a toner?

2. When should toner be used?

3. Can Manic Panic be used on pre-lightened hair?

4. When should Cellophanes be used?

5. What is Jazzing?

Answers

1. A toner is a semi-permanent hair color used to tone down unwanted color.

2. To diminish unwanted brassy tones or to change the tonality of the hair.

3. It is best on pre-lightened hair, because the resulting color is very vibrant however, you can still use on natural hair it just wont be as bold.

4. To add shine and brighten a natural hair color; Cellophanes is translucent color.

5. Jazzing is a glaze, a translucent color that can be processed under the hair dryer or without heat.

NOTES

Applications

APPLICATION TECHNIQUE VARIES. THERE are a few different ways to apply hair color: a bowl and brush, a tint bottle, or with your fingers. When doing a root touch-up, I like the brush and bowl method. Measure and pour the needed amount into the bowl and mix well with plastic fork or a tint brush. As you will notice, the tint brush has one pointed end, which is used to part the hair. Begin the part in the middle of scalp, progress from the top of head to the back of the ears. Make the part with one end of the brush, turn it around to dip into and apply the hair color. Use your other hand to restrain the hair as you continue on. The thickness of the hair determines the size of the partings the thinner the hair, the larger the partings. When working with thick hair, you will probably use more hair color and place your partings closer together. You don't need to pile on the color; a nice, even coat will do. When you get to the top of the scalp and are working in the back, try to go by feel, but look in a mirror if necessary.

If you are touching up roots and there is faded color on the rest of the hair, it is best to chunk some color through the hair shaft to the ends of hair. It helps blend the new color with the rest of the hair so it looks more natural. So you don't have a line of demarcation where one color is and another starts. I do this with all my tint touch up clients. After twenty minutes of processing, take small sections around your natural part and color those sections. If you have shorter hair, take pieces throughout your whole scalp. Leave the color on for another twenty minutes before shampooing. (If your hair is dry, don't use the mix with 20- volume developer. Instead, mix a separate batch with 5 or 10- volume developer to chunk through the hair. The key is to blend the recently colored hair with the rest of the hair.) Be sure to add shampoo around the hairline and work it into your hair before shampooing it out. This helps to remove tint from your skin.

You will not need to use the chunking technique if you're using blond formulas where you are going lighter. But if you feel the roots are not as light as the hair, and it doesn't lighten after time, mix a little bleach and comb a little in the section needed. To do this, apply a bit of product on the end of the comb, comb into the area needed, and don't comb through a second time. Apply more hair color product to the comb and repeat until you think you have enough covered. I suggest doing this technique on dried hair.

Bottle application is pretty easy, whether you're doing just the roots or all-over hair color. Mix the formula in a bottle that has measurements along its side. It is usually equal amounts of hair color to developer, but some colors have you add more developer than color. Be sure to read all instructions before starting. I suggest using a tint bottle that has a long tip and holding the hair with the other hand. (All tint bottles have a pointy tip, which is used for parting the hair going one way.) Squeeze the bottle and follow the part you just made with the bottle tip. Keep repeating this technique until you are finished with the head. If you are coloring all the hair, at this point take sections starting in front, and add to the hair shaft. Leave the ends out after you finish coloring the hair shaft, then go back and do the ends. Leave on for twenty to thirty minutes. When coloring your own hair, be sure to coat the outgrowth only, because color can build up on the hair shaft. (I'm sure you have seen those people with lighter roots and an almost black hair shaft.) If it is faded, go ahead, but I would still chunk it through. I would not use bleach in the tint bottle it tends to be too thick.

When you reapplying bleach to the hair, be careful of overlapping the product on pre- bleached hair. You never want to chunk this product through the hair if bleach is already present. It will cause damage and breakage, so be careful with touch-ups.

The cap-and-hook method is a great way to highlight or lowlight your hair or just adds a different tonality to the same level you already have. You can buy the caps at beauty supply stores open to the public. Hooks are available too, but you may have some crochet hooks lying around. There are different types of caps, but the best are the disposable types with patterns to follow. They have circles on the disposable caps to help guide you, and pre made small holes you push the crochet hook through if you want to do two different shades of color, get two caps.

When you have the cap tightly on, tied under your neck. Take your crochet hook and go in carefully not to stab you or your client, turn the crochet hook and pull out. Take your fingers and pull the hair through if it gets looped up. Go around your whole head. Pull the hair out of the center of the circle for one hair color, apply the mixed color to the hair. Process thirty to forty five minuets wash and dry the hair put the cap on again, the second cap. Now pull hair through the hole that isn't in the circle. They have pre made holes all over the cap, in the circles and out of the circles. After you complete pulling all the hair through the cap mix your hair color and apply all over the head. Make sure that cap is tight on your head, also putting a lightweight plastic cap underneath the highlight cap is cautionary. That assures that the product doesn't leak onto the scalp and other areas you don't want colored. The cap under the high light cap is a different kind, like the ones you get in hotel rooms used as shower caps. Make sure your product is somewhat thick so it does not run down your face or your clients'. Leave on for thirty to forty-five minutes. More hair comes through the bigger the hook, so if you are doing two colors you may want to use two different size hooks for a more natural look. When using just one color use two different sized crochet hooks a large and small for example to give a more natural look. Putting a light cap or plastic vegetable bag over the color you now applied will help it generate heat and process quicker. If you are using liquid colors that don't thicken up with developers, you can buy a color thickener from beauty supply. Cornstarch works in a pinch too. As with most hair color applications, gloves are a must to save your hands.

Foil technique is for the stylist already proficient with color. If you have performed this technique without the benefit of professional training, I give you credit, because this is a difficult procedure. For you stylists who don't quite get it, I will walk you through this process. You will need precut foils, available in most beauty supply stores. Just cut the length you need for long or shorter hair. You will also be using a teasing comb with a pointy end. Having the client put their head down so you can start at the crown. Make about a two-inch section running from the crown of the head to the front of the face. Weave the hair, sectioning off small portions with the tip of the comb. Fold the foil around one end of the comb, so it's held in place. Lay it on the head, place the hair that you weaved on the foil, and then paint the hair color on the foil.

Holding the hair taut on foil while brushing on the color takes practice, but you will achieve beautiful and natural results once you master it. You can also start foiling at the natural part line, and move down each side to the ear, then doing the other side, and then the back. Taking tiny weaving sections produces a more natural look. Use two or three different colors, whether you're doing highlights or lowlights. You can process the color under a dryer for ten to twenty minutes, or air process for forty-five minutes after the last foil has been placed. Remember that hair color stops processing after forty-five minutes. If you happen take forty-five minutes just to do the front, make a new batch of hair color for the back of the head.

Creative Applications

THREE-DIMENSIONAL HAIR COLORS ARE a creative way to color your hair. The process involves the application of three separate hair colors to three different areas of the head. You can do the application on pre-lightened or virgin hair. You can use a darker shade at the base of the neck, a lighter shade in the crown area, and an even lighter shade on the top of the head. Or intermix the colors all around the head, staying around the same level. I do this with semi- permanent and permanent hair colors all the time, and it turns out great when I chunk the three different hair colors that are within the same level but different tones, for instance, a level 6 light brown or dark blond. I may use a gold tone with a gold and red mix and a neutral, all similar but slightly different, or I may use all different reds, I have even done black, dark brown, and chestnut red. Three- dimensional colors are best with semi-permanent or demi-permanent colors.

Hair painting or frosting is the process of applying a tint or a mild lightener in small streaks for a sun-bleached effect. The color used and the length of time it is left on the hair determines the end result. The color can be applied with a toothbrush, small paintbrush, or comb. Make sure the product is thick, so it does not run on the hair not colored.

Ballieouging is a technique that is used when added color is needed. Let's say you have done allover color, and you want to lighten or darken the hair. You can mix some bleach or color with 20–40 volume developer, put some gloves on, take a piece of the pre-colored hair, place the new color on with your fingers, and apply formula right over the existing color. Do five to ten pieces on the top of head. Leave the mixture on the hair the last five to ten minutes for processing the original color. This will add some dimension to the color you are doing to lighten and brighten it. Ballieouging can be used with any formula, whether you want to add red to brown hair or blond to light brown hair. It is a creative way to play with hair color, so have fun it. It's a fun technique to learn and it's quite impressive to pull it out at the end of the color cycle, put it on your fingers, and chunk it through the hair before you shampoo out the hair color.

Tipping is a simple technique also used for adding dimension. Blond is the most popular, but you can tip your hair with any color, if you make sure the product is thick enough for the tipping process. With gloves on, paint the color right on the tips of the hair. At that point, have some cellophane strips or foil to wrap around tipped hair so the color does not get on the rest of the hair, tipping is best on short hair. As always, remember to do a test strip when you're unsure. Hair color is so much fun; to this day I still get excited doing beautiful hair colors. Experimenting will help you become a confident hair colorist; so let the creative juices flow!

Quiz

1. What is the best way to apply hair color to the hair, brush and bowl or tint bottle?
2. How do you do highlights on your self?
3. What is chunking?
4. How is the ballieouging technique used?
5. When is the ballieouging technique used?

Answers

1. It really is a personal preference. I mainly use the brush and bowl method.
2. By using the cap and crochet hook.
3. Chunking is a technique for blending the color of a touch-up by applying hair color to the hair shaft. Add color to ¼ to half-inch chunks of hair. Add other chucked colors intermittently throughout the hair if desired.
4. Cover the hair with one color, then place another hair color on gloved fingers and piece it through the hair from the roots to the ends, usually during the final five to fifteen minutes of developing.
5. To lighten a color that has been applied but seems too dark, or to add darkness and dimension to light hair.

Going Green

THERE ARE SO MANY different ways to color hair. In this chapter, I will go through some organic methods. If the natural lifestyle appeals to you, I have a few ideas I think you will like. Even though all these products are natural, you should still perform a patch test to make sure you're not allergic. Apply a small amount of the mixed ingredients to the inside of your wrist or to the base of your scalp. If no rash appears after twenty minutes you're good to go!

Henna

Henna is a wonderful way to color your hair. The dye itself is extracted from the leaves of the plant from the loosestrife family and ground up to a fine powder. Henna has really come a long way in recent years. Previously, there were only a few colors available, but the selection has expanded. I have had good experiences with hennas. There is little risk in trying hennas, since they will rinse out and fade away over time.

Hennas may or may not cover gray, depending on the light to dark ratio. The darker the henna the better the gray coverage. Henna was the first color I ever used. Mix it with warm water to a mud-like consistency, and pack it on your hair. It warms and bakes in, leaving the hair feeling thicker and conditioned. The warmth is very relaxing and comforting while the henna processes. Henna is a great first color for the person afraid to use other colors. Buy a few different colors, mix a little from each box to do test strands, and choose your favorite.

Citrus Hair Lightener

This treatment makes your hair sun kissed, it acts with the sunlight to quickly lighten and brighten fair hair, adding shine and shimmer.

2 tablespoons fresh lemon juice
2 tablespoons fresh lime juice
1 tablespoon lemon extract
1 teaspoon lime extract

Mix all ingredients in spray bottle shake bottle and spray all over hair, go outside and remain in sun for at least 30 minutes. Apply several times a day while outside. This application will dry hair so follow with a good conditioning treatment. Warning: keep out of eyes. Refrigerate after use discard after 1 week.*

*Frank and Lucy Fraser and Wendy Ryerson.1996. Blended Beauty.

Chamomile and Calendula Hair Lightener

These flowers help to soften and brighten your hair. Gives it a golden glow.

Botanical formula
4 cups of water
2 cups dried chamomile flowers
2 cups dried calendula flowers (pot marigold)
1 tablespoon lemon juice
1 tablespoon lemon extract

In a saucepan bring water and flowers to a boil. Reduce heat, and simmer for 45 minutes. Remove from heat and cool, stirring in lemon juice and extract. When cooled apply to hair and comb through, put plastic cap over head and leave on 40 minutes, rinse with warm water. Use every other day for lasting effects. Makes 4 cups. Shelf life: cover and refrigerate; discard after 5 days.*

Black Tea- Rosemary Rinse for Dark Brown Hair

Enhance and condition and tone your natural deep brown hair. It will also add richness and darken light brown hair.

Botanical Formula
7 bags of black tea or 2 1/2 tablespoons of loose black tea
2 tablespoons oregano leaves
2 tablespoons chopped rosemary leaves
2 cups water
1 tablespoon instant coffee
1 tablespoon lemon extract

*Frank and Lucy Fraser and Wendy Ryerson.1996. Blended Beauty.

In a saucepan over medium heat, mix the tea, oregano, and rosemary with the water. Steep for 45-50 minutes. Remove tea bags and filter out ingredients, and put into a pitcher. Add coffee and lemon extract let cool. Slowly pour over your head its best to be in the shower or bath because the solution is very thin consistency. Wrap hair in plastic for 30 minutes, rinse with warm water. Cover and refrigerate; discard after 5 days.*

Rum and Egg Build Up Remover with Shampoo

Rum and Egg is one of the classic hair combinations for removing build up from your hair. It helps to strip hair product build up from the hair leaving it silky smooth.

> 1 cup shampoo (oily or dandruff shampoo)
> 1 tablespoon white rum
> 1 whole egg
> 1 teaspoon of peppermint extract

Mix all ingredients in a blender on low, shampoo as usual. Refrigerate; discard after 3 days.*

Clove and Apple Dandruff Shampoo

This recipe is a great to exfoliate dandruff. Removes build up from oil and hair care products. Leaves your scalp feeling clean and refreshed.

> ¼ cup shampoo
> 1 tablespoon apple cider vinegar
> 3 tablespoons apple juice
> ½ teaspoon rum extract
> 6 finely ground cloves

Put all ingredients in blender, on low blend until completely mixed. Small bits of clove will remain in solution, not to worry. Shampoo as usual. Refrigerate; discard after 3 days.*

Avocado Hair Conditioner

Avocado, is conditioning and hydrating, it moisturizes the hair shaft. It adds shine and body to over stressed hair. For best results use often.

> 2 teaspoons avocado oil

*Frank and Lucy Fraser and Wendy Ryerson.1996. Blended Beauty.

2 tablespoons olive oil
2 teaspoons canola oil
2 tablespoons vegetable shortening
2 teaspoons coconut oil
2 teaspoons honey

In small saucepan warm all ingredients except the honey, remove from heat and cool, add honey and mix well. Massage through hair leave on 20 minutes, Rinse out. If coconut oil is not available use an extract added the same time as the honey.*

I have used these recipes over the years and enjoyed the homemade products; Blended Beauty is the best book on the market for natural skin and hair treatments.

*Frank and Lucy Fraser and Wendy Ryerson.1996. Blended Beauty.

Quiz

1. What is henna?

2. How do I know when to use henna?

3. Is making my own rinses and masques easy?

4. What is the shelf life of home made rinses and masques?

5. How can I create my own receipts?

Answers

1. Henna is a dye extracted from the leaves of a plant.

2. When you don't want to use chemicals on your hair.

3. It is, there are several foods that can be used from yogurt, mayonnaise, olive oil, its experimenting and trying new things.

4. I would not let it go longer than five days refrigerated.

5. It's being a scientist and experimenting with different ingredients in your kitchen. Yogurt, honey, eggs, mayonnaise and coconut milk, and many other items in your refrigerator and pantry.

NOTES

Scalp Treatments, Disorders, and Diseases

TROUBLED BY ITCHY SCALP? Tired of having those annoying white flakes on your shoulders? Let's go over some natural approaches to relieve the problems.

Dandruff, pityriasis by its scientific name, is one of the most common scalp conditions. It can result from harsh chemicals, bad shampoos, stress, and even poor circulation. Dandruff can rear its ugly head in two different forms: dry dandruff and oily dandruff. Dry dandruff is the pieces of skin that flake off the scalp and show up in your hair or on that nice black shirt you have. Oily dandruff is a waxy, greasy coating on your scalp. Dandruff also causes itchiness, so even though you may not have visible symptoms, you can still have dandruff. Dandruff is a bacterium, and through the proper use of products, you can keep it under control. When you have an oily scalp, you have an overactive sebaceous gland. A dry scalp it is under active sebaceous gland that doesn't produce enough natural oil.

The product I recommend is Paul Mitchell tea tree special shampoo, but there are a lot of other tea tree shampoos out there. If you have a bad case of dandruff, the tar shampoos work well; Neutrogena makes one I like, and Aveda has a multi-step process with oils to massage into the scalp, followed by a nice shampoo and conditioner. A stylist can provide this as a service in the salon that will benefit clients and catch dandruff before it becomes a problem for them.

Scalp massage works to free the scalp of loose, flaky skin. If your hair is long, section it in four portions, and pin it up. Take each section down at one time, and brush it with a natural boar bristle brush. Place the brush on the scalp, and roll it to the end of your hair. Repeat several times. Look in the mirror. Your scalp will be pink, and that is a good thing. You shouldn't catch your hair in the brush if you do the process correctly. Massage is also great if you are losing your hair; it stimulates the scalp by bringing blood to the surface and generates new growth. Getting one of those round scalp brushes that fits in the palm of your hand works great for short hair. A regular brush is best for longer hair. Go around your whole head making little circular patterns on the scalp, and take your time. This is best performed on dry hair. I had a client who swore he grew new hair just by massaging his scalp and using no chemicals. I met him after the fact, and he did have new growth and a full head of hair, so I'm a believer in scalp massage. You can use your fingers instead of a brush. Be consistent and patient. Get into a routine, just like brushing your hair that you can stick to for six months to a year. This procedure is also great for pattern baldness.

Sebum is produced by an overactive sebaceous gland. It is a waxy substance that kills the root of the hair by plugging it up. Scalp manipulation helps to stop the process by generating blood flow to the area.

Alopecia, or baldness, is a disease that causes hair loss. It can be caused by an infection, a disease, or genetics. There are several types of alopecia, some of which are treatable. A dermatologist may be able to help you through the process. One of my close friends has alopecia, and she does a beautiful job with her wigs and makeup. You would never know she has the disease. I am so proud that she rose above her illness to become one of the most stunningly beautiful women I know.

Quiz

1. What is dandruff?
2. Are there different types of dandruff?
3. How does massage make new hair grow?
4. What is sebum?
5. What is alopecia?

Answers

1. Dandruff is a bacterium that causes a flaky and itchy scalp.
2. There are two different types: dry dandruff that causes flaky scalp and oily dandruff that produces a waxy, greasy coating on your scalp. Both cause itchiness.
3. It stimulates the scalp by bringing blood to the surface and generating new growth.
4. It's a waxy plug that kills the root of the hair.
5. Alopecia is a disease that causes hair loss on the scalp and body. It starts with patches of hair loss around the head.

NOTES

Hair Color Corrections

COLOR CORRECTIONS ARE IMPORTANT when you need to fix your hair or someone else's. Whether your hair is drab or brassy, there are hair color corrections that can help. Let's go over some of the most popular.

If the hair is too brassy or if its highlighted hair that is level 7 or higher, I recommend that you use a toner or a permanent hair color with 5-volume developer. I would use a level 9 or 10 violet base, ash base color, depending how light your hair is. You can put this product all over the head and leave on for twenty to thirty minutes. Make sure you have your gloves on, rub the hair between two towels. Check to see where the color is in its process after fifteen minutes. If you like the results, shampoo the dye out. If you are not pleased, mush the strand back into the rest of the colored hair, and check it in another fifteen to thirty minutes. The process is usually ideal by that point. For highlighted hair, you can also isolate and color only the pieces that are too brassy. Always perform a test strand if you are unsure of the product.

If you want to revert to your natural hair color, there are a few different ways to accomplish this. If you are covering gray, and you or your client wants to stop coloring her hair, here is one way. If you are a level 7 or darker, there are a few different ways. The first method replaces permanent hair colors with semi-permanent or even demi- permanent hair color. After a while, the product will rinse out of the roots you are touching up. Don't go lower than a level 7, because anything darker can deposit on the hair and will not rinse out easily. This works well with short hair, because you will soon be cutting the old color out, at which point you should stop the semi-permanent process. When is the hair color rinses out, you will be back to your natural color.

Bleach the second way of returning hair to its natural color. If the hair has a good two to four inches of outgrowth, and the colored part of the hair is from gray to black to brown or red level 4 to 8, apply a bleach mixture with 20 or 30-volume developer to the colored section of hair. The goal is to pull all the pigment out of the hair and get it to a pale yellow color like the inside of a banana. This technique suitable for hair that's at least 75 percent gray. Shampoo out the dye, then condition and dry the hair. Then mix a formula, a light ash or beige toner or level 8 or 9 violet base hair color with a 5 or 10 volume developer. Apply it on the gray outgrowth first, and leave it on for ten minutes, then apply it to the pre-lightened hair that you have just stripped, and leave it on for another twenty minutes before shampooing and conditioning. I recommend that you trim a lot off the hair so that little of the bleached remains. It usually blends well, but as it fades, you may need to repeat the toner process. If it doesn't blend well, go a shade darker with the toner.

You may want to try two different toners and do a test strand with both of them. If you are unsure of what results you want to achieve, you can also use this process on shorter hair.

If you have too much red, you will need to apply a hair color that is darker than the natural hair and has a blue base color .You can also add blue pigment to the color to cool it down a little more. Do not use this on bleached or highlighted hair, which can turn blue in the process.

To achieve an allover lightened look on dark hair, apply a mixture of bleach and 20-volume developer to the hair shaft and the ends before adding it to the roots of the hair. Just watch it, and get it to a shade lighter than the one you want. You are not stripping all the hair color you just want to remove a few layers of pigment. The hair will lighten to a light ugly red. Shampoo, condition, and dry the hair. It's okay if it remains a bit damp. You will then mix the new color one or two levels darker with 20-volume developer, if hair is dry and damaged use a 10-volume developer and apply it to hair shaft, to the roots, then to the ends; leave it on for thirty minutes. Again, a good trim is needed to give the color a fresh, healthy, finished look.

If your hair is too ashy and drab, do just the opposite of the previous process: add warmth with red base colors or warm gold's. So many people are afraid of gold tones, but I just love them. They can warm up your whole look and put back that glow in your skin and eyes. Warm gold's can add a richer color tonality, because ashy tones are not flattering on everyone.

Bringing highlighted hair back to natural color. You will need to prime the hair first. You will add the color back to the hair the way it was stripped out. First you mix level 8 gold color with 5-volume developer, apply it all over highlighted area, process twenty five minuets, Rinse out, add conditioner rinse out, and dry. Next mix a formula level 7 or 6 red color with 5-volume developer, follow last process. Then you mix the color you want close to the natural color, usually a shade darker. Apply it with10-volume developer to the hair shaft, the scalp area, and then the ends, leave on thirty to forty five minuets shampoo and condition. A deep conditioning treatment should be done after this process. This may fade after a few month's at that time you may want to add a semi or demi color to your hair to add shine and condition.

When doing color corrections, always condition the hair well. Apply a deep conditioner, put on a cap on, and sit under the hair dryer. If you don't have a dryer, sit in the sun for fifteen minutes. If you can't be outside, clean house or exercise physical activity will warm your scalp and hair. After you shampoo and condition, rinse well, towel dry, and apply a leave-in conditioner if desired.

Quiz

1. What is color correction?

2. How is dark colored hair lightened?

3. How can two-toned hair be made all one color?

4. How should Manic Panic be removed from hair?

5. When should a drabber be used?

Answers

1. Color correction is the process of changing a disliked hair color. It can be as major as three or four steps or just using another color.

2. I recommend using hair color remover or bleach to make the hair two to three shades lighter. By applying it all over the hair watching it till it gets a shade lighter than you want. Shampoo and condition, dry the hair. You will now apply a hair color a shade or two darker than the lightened hair, using 5-10 volume developer.

3. Apply hair color remover or bleach to lighten up the darkest hair to nearly match the level of the other color, shampoo out, and dry. Apply a new hair color in the shade desired all over.

4. If it doesn't come out after a period of time, apply and leave on a color remover or bleach until the color disappears. Shampoo, dry, and apply an allover hair color in a shade or two darker.

5. Use a drabber or toner on your hair when hair is too brassy or has unwanted orange and gold tones.

NOTES

Product Knowledge

HAIR PRODUCTS ARE A billion-dollar industry. Today's products can be very costly, so I usually buy from the middle price range. Your hair type will determine the products that are best for you. This chapter will identify what works best for each hair type and suggest some of my favorite helpful products.

For fine, flyaway hair, use a volumizing shampoo or a shampoo for fine, thinning hair with no conditioner. For colored hair, however, use a volumizing conditioner. Never use moisturizing shampoo or conditioner. They will weigh down your hair so that it gets oily sooner. You can always use a leave-in spray-on conditioner if necessary. A root lifter or mousse works well also. Be careful not to over apply, which will make hair look dirty. A stylist may want to rinse the hair and start over using fewer products, and clients will appreciate someone looking after their best interests. The lightest hair sprays will work best for fine hair.

For dry, damaged hair, you need a moisturizing shampoo and conditioner or a product specified for dry and damaged hair. Always use a leave-in conditioner. Try to keep it all in the same product line. A leave-in conditioner will add more moisture and shine and help protect your hair against the elements. Some leave-in conditioners have sunscreen in them and are very helpful in protecting the hair. I would not suggest using mousse, because it contains alcohol and could further dry your hair. Use a gel for styling, and follow up with a sealer or gloss. Rub a small amount together in your hands for even distribution, then run your hands through your hair, starting on the hair shaft and avoiding the roots and scalp. Hair spray is optional, but it does contain alcohol. I find that glosses work well.

If you have colored-treated hair, make sure your products are formulated for your specific needs. The product should have this information needed on the front or back of the bottle. For normal hair, you can use just about anything, but if you are prone to fly- away or static electricity, try a glazing finishing product or a leave-in conditioner.

For men's hair, I like Pinaud-Clubman styling gel. It has a light to medium hold, and you can still run your hands through your hair when it dries. It has a masculine smell, and I have been using this product on my male clients for years with great results. For a lighter hold, I like Jerris hair tonic with oil, though it comes in an oil-free version as well. It's ideal for men (or the women who use it) with fine hair or men with naturally curly hair. It has a lightweight hold and adds shine to dull hair. You can find these products at beauty supply stores.

I switch to a new kind of shampoo and conditioner each time I use up a bottle, because hair becomes accustomed to products and will not continue to show the prime results it initially achieved. With so many wonderful products available, I like to mix things up when I go shopping.

Quiz

1. How do I find the best products for me?

2. Why is important to use shampoo formulated for color-treated hair?

3. What kind of shampoo increases the fullness of fine, thin hair?

4. What protect can protect hair from sun exposure?

5. How can dry, drab, and dull, hair become healthier?

Answers

1. Knowing your own hair type, then look at labels and buy products that fit your profile.

2. Regular shampoos may contain detergents that strip color and cause it to fade prematurely.

3. Volumizing shampoos and conditioners work best.

4. Apply a leave-in conditioner with SPF 15 throughout the day to keep your colored hair from fading.

5. Taking a cod liver pill daily increases the oils in your system, which comes out in your skin and hair. Follow with moisturizing shampoo and conditioner. You can also use a leave in conditioner, followed by a polisher or gloss for shine.

NOTES

$\mathcal{S}$alon Styles

STYLING THE HAIR PLAYS the most important part in the finished result. Whether you do nothing but finger a little gel into your hair or take the time to set and blow-dry it, you can have beautiful results. I will give you the tools to look as if you just left the salon when in fact you just left your bathroom.

Blow-drying is a good technique to add volume to fine, limp hair. Apply a mousse, a spray root lifter, or any styling product for fine, limp hair. I advise against anything heavier, like a gel, which could weigh down your hair and make it dirtier and oily sooner. When using a mousse, shake it well, spray it into your palm, apply to the root area, run it through your hair, and begin styling. Less is more when dealing with fine hair. When using a root lifter, spray directly onto the root and scalp area, lifting and spraying under the sections around your head. Again, too much product can weigh your hair down. After applying the product, get out your blow dryer, round brush, and vent brush. Brush your hair against the way that it falls, drying the root area before going over all sections of the head. Brush upward with the vent brush, and then slightly down to create a little bubble in the hair. Nestle the blow dryer in that section to fluff up the roots and create space around your scalp. The hair is fuller when it lay's back down. Now use a round brush and dry the hair shaft to the ends to complete the drying process. Longer hair may need to be pinned up and taken down to dry in sections. There is a great tool on the market for people who find it hard to coordinate this process. The combination of a blow- dryer and round brush in one tool is easy to use and widely available.

When blow-drying dry, thick hair, it's best to use a good leave-in conditioner or a gloss to take the puff out; a straightening gel works well. Again, dry the roots first with a vent brush, then go back and dry the hair shaft with a flat or round brush. Make sure the hair is taut on the brush. This pulling and stretching will keep your hair from frizzing. If a section does frizz, add a little spray-in conditioner, and pull and stretch it with the brush, and blow-dry it again. You can always flat iron your hair to get some of the bulk out, though the process is drying to the hair. If your hair is dry already, limited use of the flatiron is the best.

Setting the hair is my recommendation for those who cannot master blow-drying. Velcro rollers are available at any drugstore or beauty supply store. Twelve to fifteen rollers should be enough. Those with thick hair may need an additional package. Hair dryers to sit under are usually available at beauty supply stores for between thirty-five and fifty dollars. They may be available to order if they aren't in stock. Allowing your hair to air-dry also produces a very sexy effect. Most celebrities you see out and about with fabulous hair probably sat under a hair dryer earlier that day. Hair type and length will determine the size of roller to use. For instance, I use the biggest yellow, blue, and red Velcro rollers. My hair is naturally curly, and it can be frizzy, but I love the results setting gives me. It straightens and adds body, but most of all it gives your hair shine and luster. Your hair will look healthier, and the style can last for three to five days. Hot rollers work well if you don't have time to redo your hair. Be sure to let them cool completely before taking them out, or the curl will flop. Similarly, make sure to completely dry your hair when using a blow- dryer. Even a little dampness can cause frizz. Take the extra few minutes, and make sure it's done correctly. Try new ways to roll the hair to get different results. When you're done, add a little serum or gloss to add even more shine and give a finished look. For fine hair, spray shine is much lighter.

Find the hair spray that is best suited to your hair goals. If you like a soft look that you can run your fingers through, get a soft hold. If you want hair that's as hard as a helmet, get hard or strong hold. Whatever finishing product you select, remember that overuse can cause buildup that requires a detoxifying shampoo, such as the kind swimmers use to remove chlorine from their hair.

If you are the kind of person who doesn't want to spend much time on hair care, make sure you communicate this so your stylist can give you a wash-and-wear cut. If your hair is naturally curly, leave-in conditioners, glosses, and curl enhancers can enhance its texture. You don't have to hide it in a ponytail. Your hair can look beautiful and healthy whatever its type.

Quiz

1. It is so hard to manage a brush and a blow- dryer at the same time; is there any tool that can make it easier?

2. How can I avoid getting Velcro rollers stuck in my hair?

3. I have this white film on my hair. What is it from?

4. What should I do when my hair frizzes?

5. I am a man who gets flyaway hair during the day. Is there anything I can use besides hair spray?

Answers

1. A helpful tool that combines a brush and a blow- dryer works well.

2. They even get stuck in my hair sometimes. Try to avoid placing the rollers against the scalp, and add a clippie to hold the rollers in place.

3. Hairspray builds up from cheap products or overuse. A detoxifying shampoo with stripping agents is the best way to remove it.

4. Get a good moisturizing shampoo and conditioner, and use a de-frizz serum or a gloss. Look at the product label to determine whether it should be applied to wet or dry hair.

5. My favorite product for men is Jerris hair tonic. It's lightweight and keeps the hair looking shiny and healthy.

NOTES

Final Thought

IT WAS A TRUE joy to write this book. I wish you all great luck in your hair color endeavors. Don't be afraid to go beyond your comfort zone and take a risk every once in awhile. Our "mistakes" can produce some beautiful results. Experiment, have fun, and be creative. The best colorists I know are the most creative people.

It's important to have all the developers if you are a stylist getting into a new hair color line, but the average person looking to color hair at home doesn't need to purchase all the levels 1 through 10. Buy every other level, because you can mix a 4 and a 6 to get a level 5, for example. The most important advice I can give you is to have fun. Also remember do a patch test on your skin if you feel you may be allergic to a product, and make sure to perform a patch test on your hair before trying a new color.

Remember to love the gifts God gave you. We all have beautiful hair, we just need to take the time to care for and style it. Everyone can have salon beautiful hair with the correct techniques and products. Thank you for letting me into your world. Good luck!

GLOSSARY

activator. A chemical used to increase the speed at which an oil or cream lightener develops.

allergy test. A test to for allergies to a product, it can be performed by applying a small amount of color to the base of the neck for ten to twenty minutes.

chunking. A process performed by adding color to the hair shaft and ends in segments. Usually used for blending tint touch-ups or adding dimension to drab hair.

depth of color. Describes the degree of a color in a range from dark to light.

developer. A chemical that you mix with hair color. Made of two parts hydrogen and two parts oxygen.

drabber. A product to remove brassiness and orange and gold tones from hair.

dye back. Dyeing the hair back to its original color.

henna. A vegetable-based hair substance that colors and stains the hair.

holidays. Areas of hair that were missed when applying color.

level. Depth of color from darkness to light.

lightener retouch. Applying lightener to hair that has grown since the last color application.

line of demarcation. A line created when color is overlapped on previously colored hair.

metallic dye. A coloring substance that relies on metallic salts to produce a coating action on the hair shaft. Better known as color restores.

overlapping. Applying hair color to an area that has already been colored.

oxidation. The chemical reaction that occurs when hair colors and developers are mixed and hydrogen peroxide releases oxygen.

patch test. A test to preview hair color, performed by coloring a small section of hair underneath the top layer.

permanent hair color. A color that penetrates into the cortex layer of the hair and remains until grown out or cut out.

powdered lighteners. Also known as "bleach." Used for tipping, streaking, frosting,

painting, and touching up hair.

retouch. The application of color to hair that has grown out since the last coloring application.

Semi - permanent hair color. A hair color that coats and slightly penetrates the hair.

streaking. Technique that involves lightening small or large segments of the hair. Good for accenting around the face.

single application. The process of tinting hair without pre-lightening it.

soap cap. A combination of tint, developer, and shampoo that is applied to restore color that may have faded from the hair. Usually applied during the final five to fifteen minutes of the color developing.

temporary hair color. A rinse that coats the hair and washes out easily.

tint back. Tinting the hair back to its natural hair color.

tone. The degree of hair color from warm to cool. Tonal values are red, gold, blue, violet, and green. The base of all hair colors.

toner. A semi-permanent hair color applied after hair has been lightened.

vegetable dyes. Dyes that derive their basic ingredients from plants. They color the hair by coating the shaft and staining the cuticle.

virgin tint. The application of tint to hair that has never been colored or lightened.

HAIR COLOR FORMULAS

HAIR COLOR FORMULAS

HAIR COLOR FORMULAS

Breinigsville, PA USA
31 March 2010
235262BV00003B/189/P